I0802936

Medieval Life

by Grace Hansen

Abdo THE MIDDLE AGES Kids

Abdo Kids Jumbo is an Imprint of Abdo Kids
abdobooks.com

abdobooks.com

Published by Abdo Kids, a division of ABDO, P.O. Box 398166, Minneapolis, Minnesota 55439.
Copyright © 2026 by Abdo Consulting Group, Inc. International copyrights reserved in all countries.
No part of this book may be reproduced in any form without written permission from the publisher.
Abdo Kids Jumbo™ is a trademark and logo of Abdo Kids.

Printed in the United States of America, North Mankato, Minnesota.

052025

092025

THIS BOOK CONTAINS RECYCLED MATERIALS

Photo Credits: AdobeStock, Alamy, Getty Images, Granger Collection, pngTree, Shutterstock

Production Contributors: Teddy Borth, Jennie Forsberg, Grace Hansen
Design Contributors: Candice Keimig, Pakou Moua

Library of Congress Control Number: 2024947610

Publisher's Cataloging-in-Publication Data

Names: Hansen, Grace, author.

Title: Medieval life / by Grace Hansen

Description: Minneapolis, Minnesota : Abdo Kids, 2026 | Series: The Middle Ages | Includes online resources and index.

Identifiers: ISBN 9798384905325 (lib. bdg.) | ISBN 9798384906025 (ebook) | ISBN 9798384906377 (Read-to-me ebook)

Subjects: LCSH: Civilization, Medieval--Juvenile literature. | Social history--Juvenile literature. | Middle Ages--Juvenile literature. | Medieval history--Juvenile literature. | Dark Ages--Juvenile literature.

Classification: DDC 940.1--dc23

Table of Contents

The Middle Ages

The Middle Ages, or medieval period, was a time in European history. It lasted from about 500 to 1500 CE. Daily life was very different during this time.

Europe
Asia
Africa

Medieval Villages

What a person's day looked like depended on who they were and where they lived. Medieval villages were in **rural** areas. Villages were mainly filled with peasants.

7

Peasants were poor farmers. They lived in huts made of wood. Their animals lived with them. They woke very early in the mornings to farm the land.

Medieval Towns

Towns were located near major roads and **waterways**. They were often built around castles. Towns were busy, smelly, and noisy places.

Craftspeople, such as **cobblers** and cloth makers, lived in towns. Towns were also filled with merchants. Merchants bought and sold goods.

Cobbler

The town's poorest families lived in small, one-room homes. Several families may have even lived in the same house. Wealthy families lived in larger, more comfortable homes with many rooms.

Wealthy home
One-room home

Children

Children born in medieval times were lucky to survive into adulthood. Boys began to learn a **trade** at age 7. Girls learned to cook and make clothes. Children from wealthier families attended school.

Food

Bread, vegetables, and dairy products were common foods to eat in medieval times. Peasants enjoyed **preserved** meats for special occasions. Wealthier people often ate fresh fish and pork.

Entertainment

People in medieval times enjoyed telling stories and singing songs. They also liked music and dancing. Popular games included cards, dice, and guessing games.

Clothing of Medieval Times

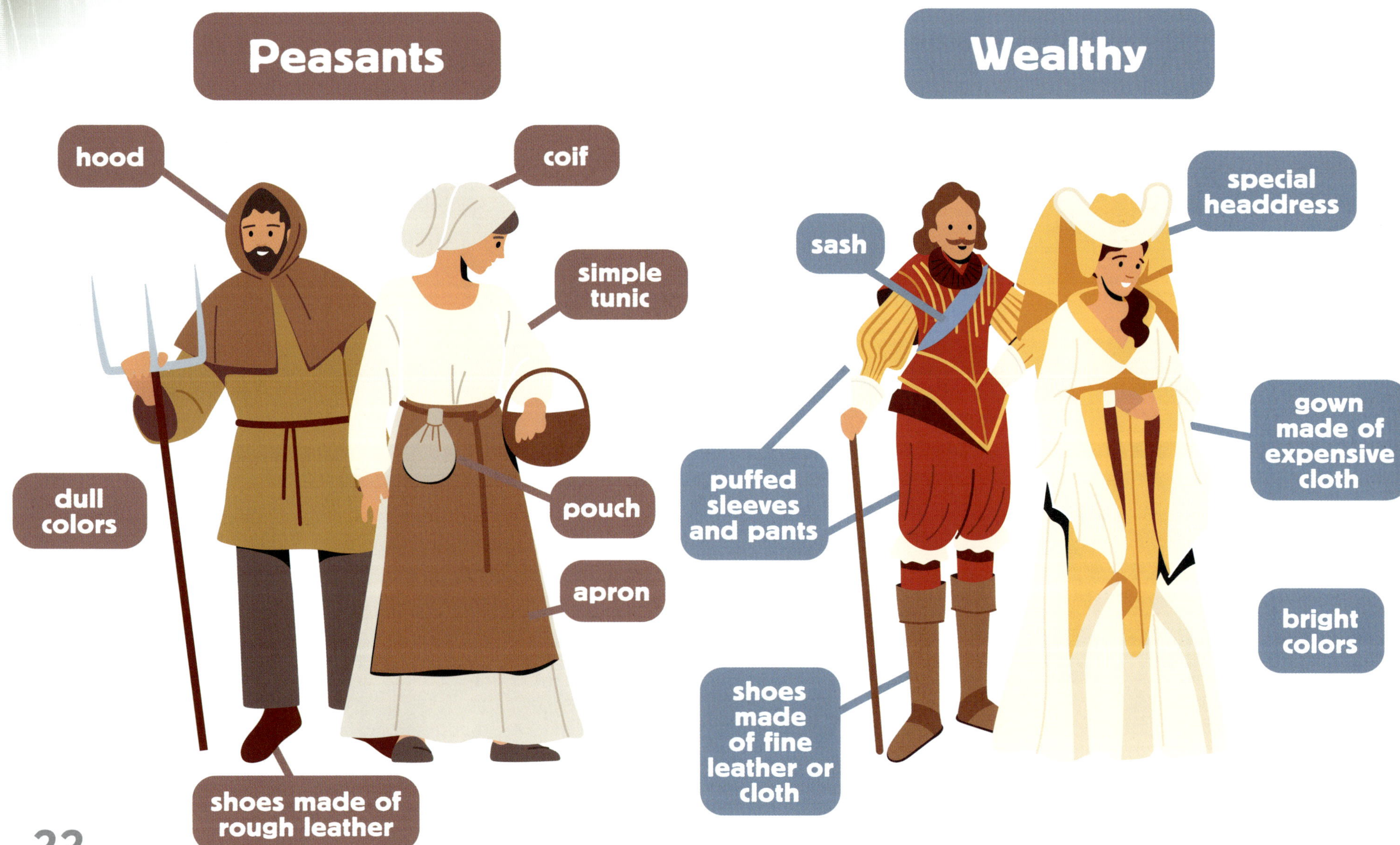

Glossary

cobbler – a person who makes or fixes shoes or boots.

preserved – prepared (as vegetables, fruits, or meats) to be kept for future use.

rural – having to do with country life.

trade – a job that involves a certain skill.

waterway – a long body of water large enough for boats to travel on.

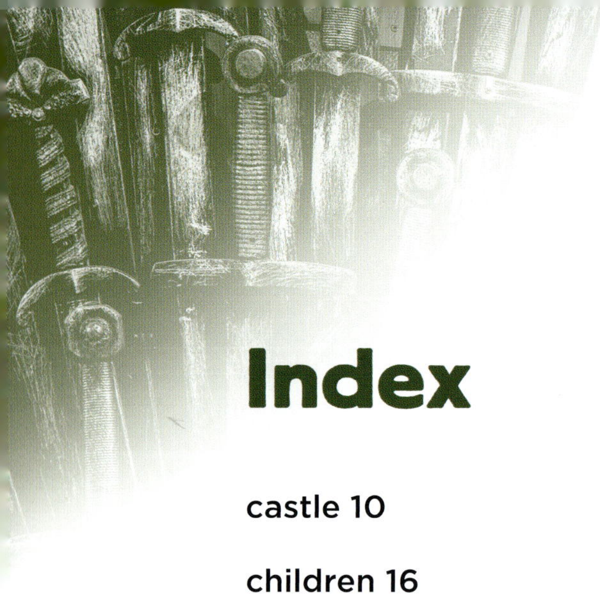

Index

Abdo Kids ONLINE
ABDO
FREE! ONLINE MULTIMEDIA RESOURCES

Visit abdokids.com to access crafts, games, videos, and more!

Use Abdo Kids code TMK5325 or scan this QR code!